Osterley Park House

A NATIONAL TRUST PROPERTY

ADMINISTERED BY

THE VICTORIA AND ALBERT MUSEUM

THIS GUIDE IS SPONSORED BY **Mobil**

Osterley Park House

JOHN HARDY · MAURICE TOMLIN

VICTORIA AND ALBERT MUSEUM

Published by the
Victoria and Albert Museum
London SW7 2RL

©The Trustees of the
Victoria and Albert Museum, 1985

Design by Patrick Yapp

Photography by Ken Jackson, Jeremy Whitaker and
Fritz von der Schulenberg

Printed in Great Britain by Balding + Mansell Limited,
Wisbech, Cambs

ISBN 0948 107 146

FRONT COVER: Osterley Park House portico showing the ceiling.

REVERSE OF COVER/HALF-TITLE PAGE: The Child's family crest embroidered on the valance of the state bed.

FRONTISPIECE/TITLE PAGE: Adam's semi-circular green house, with stable block behind.

BACK COVER: The east front of Osterley Park House.

CONTENTS

INTRODUCTION

Visiting Osterley Park is a journey through a late eighteenth-century recreation of the classical world. Every decorative motif, statue or wall-painting was chosen because it aroused images of Greek and Roman architecture or literature in the visitor's mind. Most of us today have not been brought up to the same familiarity with the classics, and architectural publications like Robert Wood's *Ruins of Palmyra* (1753) are scarcely the hot news they once were. So if the cleverness and subtlety of Osterley Park House is to be appreciated, we must have these allusions pointed out to us and explained; that is why this guide dwells at length on the ornament of each room.

A visitor to the house in the 1770s wrote, 'I was told that the above building cost one hundred and thirty thousand pounds; you will suppose the whole is something extraordinary, when I tell you that it claims the attention of the King and every great personage in England.'

Whereas most other houses have been altered or redecorated so that it is exceedingly difficult to envisage how they looked originally, Osterley is remarkable in that it still boasts much of its eighteenth-century decor and retains its grand Georgian furnishings. Indeed the antechamber of the state apartment created by the banker Robert Child and his architect Robert Adam in the 1770s is one of the few rooms in the world to remain in its entirety as it was in the eighteenth century: the furnishings that had been introduced later were removed in 1949, so that the eighteenth-century arrangements could once again be presented without later accretions.

The house and park were generously given to the National Trust in 1949 by the Earl of Jersey. They were subsequently leased to the Ministry of Works, now the Department of the Environment, which maintains the property. The furniture, on the other hand, was purchased by the nation and placed in the custody of the Victoria and Albert Museum which administers the house itself. The park is administered by the Royal Parks section of the Department of the Environment, and at present the National Trust, under the guidance of Mr E Fawcett, are carrying out a scheme to restore some of its eighteenth-century features. The present guide has been written by John Hardy and Maurice Tomlin under my general supervision and in collaboration with our colleagues.

We are very grateful indeed to Lord Jersey for the help he has given us on many occasions in furthering our understanding of Osterley – a house of which he is very fond and of which, for our part, we are very proud.

SIMON JERVIS
Deputy Keeper of Furniture and Interior Design,
Victoria and Albert Museum, 1985.

The east front of Osterley Park House across the lake.

BELOW: The stable block.

OPPOSITE: A map by
Moses Glover, 1638, from
the collection of the Duke of
Northumberland.

The stable block to the north of the house was built by Sir Thomas Gresham in the 1570s, but there have been considerable alterations to the doors and windows in later years. The clock in the central turret was supplied by Richard Street in 1714, and its bell is inscribed 'Thomas Swaine made me in 1753'. The Tuscan porch also dates from the 1750s, when Chambers designed the interior of the east wing, basing it on the engraving of the Somerset House stables in Isaac Ware's *Designs of Inigo Jones*, 3rd edition 1756. The coach yard was paved in 1783.

Chambers assisted with the layout of the pleasure gardens to the west of the stable block with its lawns, serpentine gravel paths and beds of evergreen shrubs. He also designed the Doric garden temple, which is dedicated to Pan, the god of flocks and herds, who ruled over Arcadia, the pastoral paradise of poets. The interior walls are stuccoed with medallion portraits of two British worthies representing the Arts and Sciences: the architect Colen Campbell (d. 1729) author of *Vitruvius Britannicus*, 1715, suspended below a laurel wreath, and Sir Isaac Newton (d. 1727), accompanied by a caduceus or

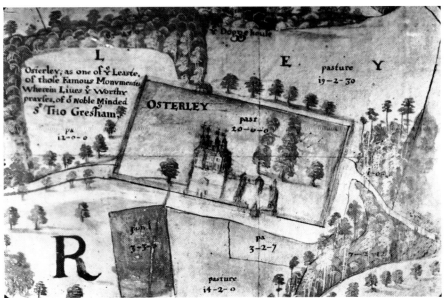

TOP: The Doric temple.

BOTTOM: The interior of the Doric temple.

OPPOSITE: Plan of the grounds.

magician's wand. The other medallion heads symbolise the seasons and their scroll frames with crossed branches incorporate animal heads, which represent the elements. In Robert Child's day the temple was furnished with chairs and a mahogany dining table.

In 1763 Adam erected nearby a great orangery with Grecian Doric columns (burnt down in 1950), and his semi-circular greenhouse, ornamented with stucco medallions of festive figures[1], was built in the mid 1770s. From this garden a path leads in a broad sweep to the top of the lake in the south-west corner of the park, giving glimpses of the west front of the house through clumps of trees and old oaks. The magnificent cedars by the lake were planted by Robert Child, and nearby is a mound which conceals the former ice-house.

In the eighteenth century the house was approached from the south-east corner of the park through the Wyke Green entrance lodges, designed by Adam in 1775, and the main drive swept through meadows beyond the principal lake to approach the stable block. A 'Roman' bridge built by Chambers across the lower lake in the 1750s led to the Aviary[2] in the north-eastern corner of the park and the London to Oxford road.

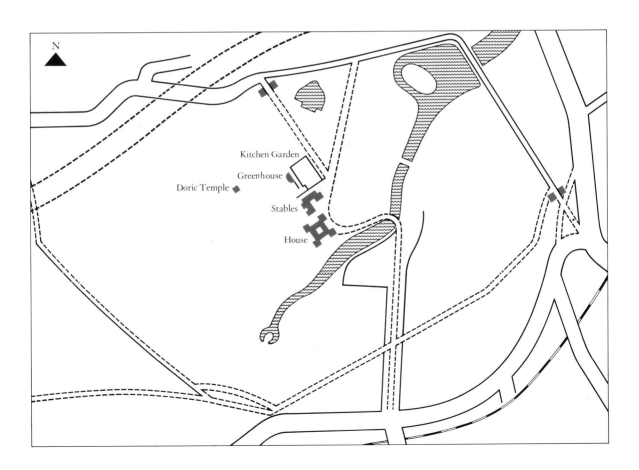

The principal ornament of the park is the house itself, a rectangular red brick mansion, with a stone balustrade cornice, and corner turrets with ogee cupolas terminating in pine-cone finials supported by 'Roman' acanthus. The neo-classical 'temple' portico creates a picturesque effect, when viewed from a distance, and was originally intended to support statues, including one of Minerva, goddess of the Arts. The west front, designed by Chambers, has a central bay, surmounted by a pediment, and its Doric entrance door is adapted from an engraving in Isaac Swan, *A Collection of Designs in Architecture*, 1757, with foliage added to the capitals. The elliptical staircase with railings designed by Adam incorporates a garden vestibule, decorated in his 'Etruscan' style.

In the eighteenth century the house and garden were inseparable and interwoven. The corner turrets provided belvederes for the appreciation of the park, the garden temples and greenhouses served as outside rooms, while the plants and flowers furnished the house. Osterley is one of the grand Middlesex villas which were created for recreation, entertainment and for the enjoyment of the arts.

OPPOSITE TOP:
The great orangery.

OPPOSITE BOTTOM: The semi-circular greenhouse.

BELOW: The west front of Osterley Park House.

The east front of Osterley
Park House.

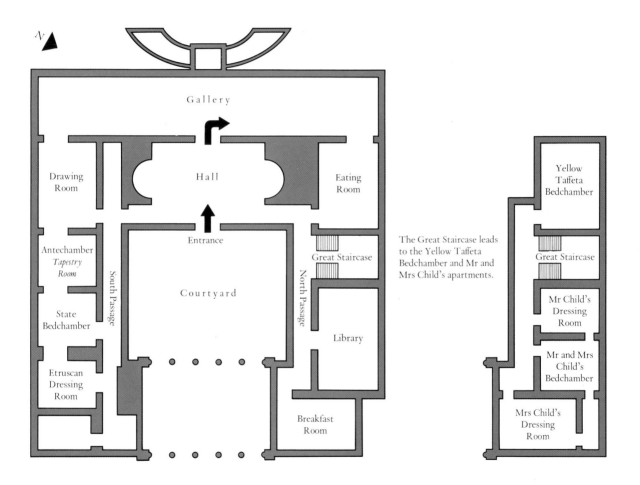

N

Gallery

Hall

Drawing
Room

Eating
Room

Entrance

Antechamber
*Tapestry
Room*

South Passage

Courtyard

North Passage

Great Staircase

State
Bedchamber

Library

Etruscan
Dressing
Room

Breakfast
Room

The Great Staircase leads
to the Yellow Taffeta
Bedchamber and Mr and
Mrs Child's apartments.

Yellow
Taffeta
Bedchamber

Great Staircase

Mr Child's
Dressing
Room

Mr and Mrs
Child's
Bedchamber

Mrs Child's
Dressing
Room

THE ENTRANCE

Eagles with adders in their beaks, the Child family crest, guard the great flight of steps leading to the entrance court. This is screened by a 'transparent' temple portico derived from reconstructions of the ancient Portico of Septimius Severus, Rome and was designed by Robert Adam in 1763. The Ionic volutes of the columns are inspired by the engraving of the capitals of the Erechtheum on the Acropolis, which was published in James Stuart and Nicolas Revett, *The Antiquities of Athens*, 1762, but Adam, following the Roman concept of 'variety' in architecture, has substituted a fluted neck-band for the original one of palmettes and anthemia. The anthemia were adapted instead for the entablature of the entrance door. Horace Walpole considered the double porticoed entrance to be 'as noble as the Propyleum at Athens', the entrance gateway to the Acropolis. However, the primary source would appear to have been the Propyleum of the Temple of the Sun, engraved in Robert Wood's, *The Ruins of Palmyra*, 1753, which also provided the inspiration for the plasterwork of the soffit with its octagon compartment and sunflower rosettes. The laurel-wreathed medallion on the façade of the pediment portrays a Roman marriage, and is flanked by tripod torchères supported by arabesque griffins. These mythical beasts were associated with fire in antiquity, and serve to guard the entrance to the family hearth at Osterley.

OPPOSITE: The portico.

RIGHT: The portico soffit.

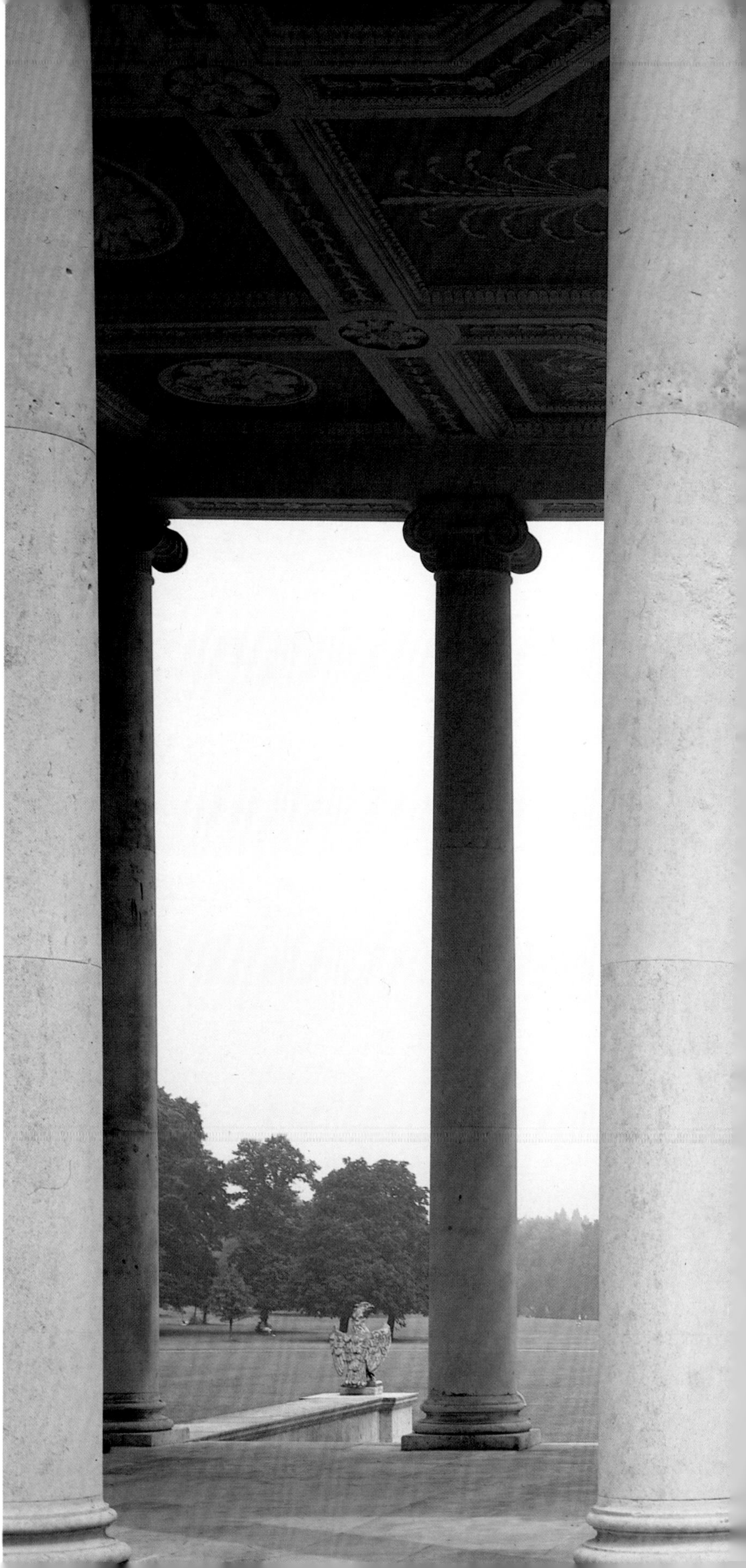

THE HALL

The hall was designed by Adam in 1767, and has stucco decoration by the firm of Joseph Rose (1723–80), grisaille paintings by Giovanni Battista Cipriani (1727–85), and a stone floor inlaid with slate. The giant pilasters lining the walls have capitals inspired by those of the Emperor Diocletian's Palace at Spalato, which Adam had studied in 1757. They help to create a 'triumphal arch' effect at the ends of the room where chimney-pieces, bearing the Child family crest, are recessed in great alcoves. The alcoves have coffered ceilings with octagon compartments and rosettes inspired by those of the Basilica of Maxentius in Rome, and the wall niches contain Roman statues. Ceres, goddess of agriculture and plenty, stands at the north end, and appears again in a triumphal chariot painted in imitation of an antique bas-relief above the mantelpiece. The harvest-goddess is accompanied by the wine-god Bacchus, who holds a thyrsus (a staff tipped with a pine cone) and rides in a festive procession with satyrs and maenads above the opposite mantelpiece. These two deities are intended to remind the viewer that, as the classical poet Virgil wrote in his *Georgics*, Man, having fallen from the Golden Age, was rescued by Ceres, who taught him how to till the earth with a plough, while Bacchus taught him to cultivate the vine. Next to Ceres is a statue of Hercules, god of labourers, holding the golden apples which he had seized from the garden of the Hesperides. Together, these statues signify 'Abundance through labour', which was a favourite Georgian theme. The stucco panels of Roman arms and

LEFT: The hall. ABOVE: The Triumph of Bacchus.

armour are inspired by the antique marble trophies of Octavianus Augustus (Trophies of Marius) in Rome, and may suggest that, when arms are laid aside, agriculture can flourish.

Osterley was conceived as a Pantheon of the Arts and Sciences, and the statues at the south end of the hall represent Minerva, goddess of the arts, and Apollo, god of poetry and music, while the grisaille medallion painted above the door depicts a British worthy, the scientist, Sir Isaac Newton, (d. 1727). The bronze vases are small-scale Italian replicas of the Borghese and Medici marble vases. These famous antique vases provided the inspiration for the other marble vases, which are attributed to the sculptor Joseph Wilton. One pair with satyr mask handles is carved with bacchanalian children. The other pair, with female masks, is carved with merfigures, depicting the Triumph of Galatea and the Triumph of Venus.

Although the hall would have served for the occasional grand banquet, it is treated like a Roman *vestibulum*, which marked the transition between the exterior and interior of the house and was often adorned with captured arms together with statues and flowers. Here at Osterley, flower-pots were placed on painted stands in the window bays, and the benches opposite were designed by Adam, in the form of scroll-ended window stools, ornamented with sacrificial rams' heads.[3]

BELOW: The overdoor medallion of Sir Isaac Newton.

OPPOSITE TOP LEFT: Apollo, god of poetry and music.

OPPOSITE TOP RIGHT: The south aspe of the hall.

OPPOSITE BOTTOM LEFT: Trophy panel in the hall.

OPPOSITE BOTTOM RIGHT: Plaster trophies on the west wall.

THE GALLERY

The 130 foot long gallery, designed by Chambers, occupies the entire west front of the house and originally had Venetian windows at the ends giving views over the park in three directions. Chambers took his designs for the 'Ionic' entrance door and the entablatures of the smaller doors from an engraving of Inigo Jones's (1573–1652) Somerset House chapel, published in Isaac Ware, *Designs of Inigo Jones*, 3rd edition, 1756. The principal ornament of the room is the scrolling 'Roman' acanthus. This is enriched with baskets of flowers on the plaster cornice, and wreathed with laurel on the mantelpieces, whose female 'term' supports derive from the sculpted figures that served in antiquity to mark boundaries of property. The frames of the mahogany seat furniture, which are designed to correspond with the mantelpiece 'terms' and the 'laurel-leaf' chair-rail, are attributed to John Linnell (1729–96), cabinet-maker of Berkeley Square. The decoration of the room was altered in 1767, when Adam filled in the Venetian windows, hung the room with pea-green in place of the original blue paper of 1759, and commissioned two long sofas, which, like the rest of the seat furniture, were upholstered in pea-green damask. Rubens's portrait of George Villiers, first Duke of Buckingham, on horseback was hung at the north end of the gallery, and facing it was a version of Van Dyck's portrait of Charles I on horseback. The gallery served to display some forty paintings, chiefly religious subjects and landscapes, and included two paintings by Claude Lorraine, which hung above the mantelpieces in the eighteenth century. The paintings would have been reflected in the huge pier glasses, which were designed by Adam in 1771, and alternate with large girandoles, whose arabesque female figures hold garlands of laurel. The Chinese items, comprising lacquer tea-tables, porcelain and mother-of-pearl pagodas and sampans, were all displayed in the window piers in the eighteenth century.

Four of the window bays were furnished with mahogany tables for plants. A set of green and white 'rout' chairs with cane seats, and four ormolu floral wall-lights above the mantelpiece complete the furnishing of the room as listed in the inventory drawn up by Linnell on the death of Robert Child in 1782.

The long gallery.

ABOVE: Gallery girandole.

RIGHT: The gallery
chimneypiece.

When his grand-daughter Sarah Sophia, Countess of Jersey (1785–1867) came to live at Osterley in 1804, she transformed the gallery into a living room and hung it with a number of family portraits. The new fashion for comfort and convenience was recorded by an American named Louis Simond, who visited the house in the early nineteenth century and commented that 'tables, sofas and chairs were studiously *derangés* about the fire-places and in the middle of the rooms, as if the family had just left them. Such is the modern fashion of placing furniture carried to an extreme, as fashions are always, that the apartments of a fashionable house look like an upholsterer's or cabinet-maker's shop.' By the end of the century the room accumulated more and more furniture and was described by Henry James as 'a cheerful upholstered avenue into another century'. In 1899 the great sofas were covered in floral needlework bearing the Child-Villiers family coat of arms together with the marigold, the emblem of Child's Bank.

The family picture collection was removed in 1949, and only the two views of the park painted by Anthony Devis were purchased for the house and hang above the mantelpieces. The remainder of the paintings are lent by the Trustees of the Victoria and Albert Museum, with the exception of the two large paintings by Sebastiano Ricci (1662–1743), which were acquired by George III from Consul Smith in Venice, and have been graciously placed on permanent loan at Osterley by Her Majesty the Queen.

ABOVE: The gallery at the end of the nineteenth century.

OPPOSITE: Two views of Osterley Park by Anthony Devis (1729–1816).

THE EATING ROOM

The traditional iconography of a banqueting room has always been to do with wine, and therefore with the god Bacchus. This one is no exception. The design of the ceiling plasterwork, with its bacchic emblems and sacrificial instruments, is attributed to William Chambers. The central rosette is framed by an oval hop-leaf garland and crossed with vine-wreathed thyrsi, while grape-clustered vines entwine an oval band of reeds and tie in corner roundels bearing wine ewers, sheathed knives and other sacrificial instruments. Bacchanalian boys play with goats among the vines on the cornice frieze, which is inspired by the pilaster ornament engraved in Robert Wood's, *Ruins of Baalbek*, 1757. The Doric chimneypiece with sacrificial skulls was designed by Chambers and executed by the sculptor Joseph Wilton in the late 1750s. The ceiling and walls were picked out in pink and green in 1767, when Adam completed the decoration and furnishing of the room. The stucco wall-panels of scrolling acanthus foliage were inspired by the seventeenth-century stucco in the Villa Pamphili in Rome and incorporate brightly coloured roundels of a Roman marriage, a wedding feast, the birth of a baby (based on 'The birth of the poet Lucan' engraved in Bernard de Montfaucon, *Antiquity Explained*, 1721–25) and the sacrifice of a ram in thanksgiving. The rectangular tablets depict festive scenes of nymphs with satyrs, who, according to the classical poets, were responsible for the education of Bacchus. The overmantel painting, by Cipriani, portrays Ceres as goddess of plenty with maidens offering sacrifices and singing her praises to the accompaniment of a lyre.

The classical *capricci* at either end of the room depict Turkish figures dancing among classical ruins and figures sporting in a decayed Roman bath. They were executed in 1767 by the Italian artist Antonio Zucchi (1726–95), who was employed by Adam as his principal decorative painter. They are in the style of the French artist Charles Louis Clérisseau, who was artistic tutor to the Adam brothers while they were in Italy, and who visited London in 1766, shortly after painting a picturesque 'ruin room' at Trinità dei Monti, Rome. Zucchi also painted the overdoors with female figures representing the continents. Europe appears in a triumphal chariot, at the sideboard end,

The eating room.

(a)

(b)

(c)

(d)

OPPOSITE TOP LEFT:
Ceiling central rose with
vine-wreathed thyrsi.

OPPOSITE TOP RIGHT:
Ceiling roundel bearing
sacrificial instruments.

ABOVE: Roundels depicting
(a) a Roman marriage, (b) a
wedding feast, (c) the birth
of a baby and (d) the sacrifice
of a ram in thanksgiving.

OPPOSITE BOTTOM: The
Doric chimneypiece.

beside a Temple, which implies that she was the cradle, if not of Christianity, at least of the Church. The horses and soldiers allude to her supremacy in war, and the cornucopia and objects symbolising the arts and sciences signify her leadership in the arts of peace.

The Doric sideboard pedestals support vases with satyr-mask handles, and flank the sideboard table with its Grecian key-fret frieze ornamented with paterae and rams' heads. The vases are lead-lined to hold water and this was piped to taps in the pedestals, which are also fitted out as pot-cupboards. Gold and silver vessels and plates would have been displayed on the sideboard, while a huge silver wine-cooler stood underneath it. The tables beneath the oval pier glasses are designed to correspond with the sideboard table and have floral marble tops of 'antique' mosaic work. Apollo's classical lyre forms the splats of the mahogany dining chairs, which are upholstered in crimson leather matching the damask festoon curtains. At the time this room was created it was not yet customary to keep a large dining table permanently in the room: instead, a number of mahogany folding tables were brought in as required and some of these are stored in the adjoining corridor.

OPPOSITE: The sideboard table and pedestals.

BELOW LEFT: Chinese plate with the family crest.

BELOW RIGHT: Detail of 'antique' mosaic work.

OVERLEAF: The eating room.

THE LIBRARY

The ceiling, designed by Adam in 1766, has broad polychrome bands, which frame a roundel and rectangular panels of low relief plasterwork on a light grey ground, and the green corner spandrels are ornamented with arabesque sphinxes. The walls, which are lined with bookcases, are treated in like manner with decorative plasterwork on a grey ground inset with brightly coloured paintings, executed by Zucchi. *Britannia encouraging and rewarding the Arts and Sciences* is portrayed above the door, and the principal decoration of the room alludes appropriately to the Arts and Sciences. Between the plaster medallions of the Greek poets Homer and Hesiod and the Roman authors Horace and Cicero are painted (on the left) *Apollo and Minerva on Mount Parnassus in the company of the Muses*: the Muses, the goddesses of artistic inspiration, are listening to Apollo, god of poetry and music, playing a lyre, which was used by Greeks for accompanying song and recitation; and (on the right) *Plato and his Disciples*. The mantelpieces are carved with arabesque boys supporting an orrery, which is emblematic of the Sciences. The ornamental painting (at the west end) depicts *Anacreon sacrificing to the Graces*, and this is flanked by *Pericles and Socrates hearing Aspasia*, who was a philosopher renowned for her skill in politics, and *Catullus writing an Epitaph for the Death of his Mistress's Bird*. The reference to the famous Latin poem by Catullus is no doubt connected with the Childs' love of birds and their aviary of exotic birds. The poetess depicted in the other overmantel painting is *The Matron, Sappho, writing the Odes dictated by Love*, and this is flanked by *The Muse of Ovid delivering a pin taken from the wing of Love*. Here the Muse, who serves as the poet's inspiration, is giving Ovid a pen made from the pin feather of Cupid's wing. On the right is *Virgil reading his works to Augustus and Octavia when he comes to speak of Marcellus, Augustus breaks into tears and Octavia faints*. The painting in the centre window pier portrays *Pythagoras restoring birds and fishes to their former freedom*. This is flanked by *Aristippus and his companions driven on shore after being shipwrecked and by some mathematical lines on the sand know that the land is inhabited*, while (on the right) *Mitellus, a Philosopher and General of the Roman Armies, orders a marble crow on the tomb of his master, Diodorus, because he taught him to chatter and not*

The east end of the library.

ABOVE: *Britannia encouraging and rewarding the Arts and Sciences.*

BELOW: One of the pedimented bookcases.

OPPOSITE: *The Matron, Sappho, writing the Odes dictated by Love* depicted in the overmantel painting.

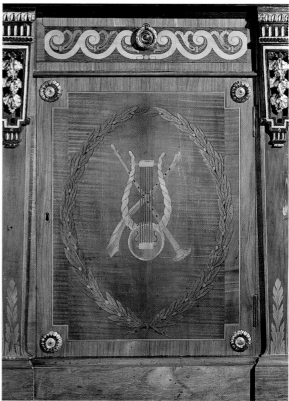

to reason. The suite of marquetry furniture comprising a desk, pair of writing tables and eight armchairs is mounted with ormolu in the French *goût grec* style and has been attributed to the workshops of John Linnell, *c.* 1768. Apollo's lyre, symbol of lyric poetry, forms the splats of the armchairs. It also appears as part of the trophy of music inlaid on the pedestal desk together with trophies of the other arts of Architecture, Painting, and Sculpture. The ormolu medallions, inspired by classical gems, which ornament the chair splats, are particularly appropriate as Robert Child collected antique coins and medals and originally kept a medal cabinet in the library.

A printed catalogue of Robert Child's superb and magnificently bound library was published in 1771. A collection of over two thousand books had been acquired by Francis Child in 1756 from the estate of Bryan Fairfax (d. 1749), and this formed the nucleus, while further books were purchased with the advice of the Rev Dr Winchester. He was tutor to the Child family, and began the book catalogue which was eventually completed by the Rev Dr Morell (1703–84). This famous classical scholar of Eton and King's College, Cambridge may also have assisted Robert Child with the subject matter for the decorative paintings in the library. Some of the books were sold in 1881.

ABOVE: Trophies of Painting and Music inlaid on the desk.

OPPOSITE: The marquetry furniture in the library.

THE BREAKFAST ROOM

The design of the plasterwork ceiling with its entwined acanthus foliage, and the mantelpiece, which is similarly decorated, is attributed to Chambers. The room was redecorated by Adam in the 1770s, when the walls were painted yellow with blue *papier-mâché* borders and hung with paintings. Among the forty-one paintings listed here in 1782 was Cotes's portrait of Mrs Child, which hung above the mantelpiece. The elegant pier glasses with term figures, cupids and vase finials were designed by Adam in 1777 as part of a unified composition en suite with the tables, which support alabaster slabs. The mahogany lyre-splat armchairs, which are attributed to Linnell, were originally upholstered in Mrs Child's own needlework. The pembroke table is probably the one listed in the 1782 inventory. There was also a harpsichord (probably the one by Kirkman, which is still in the possession of Lord Jersey) and a pair of glass lustres (those displayed on the tables are lent by the Victoria and Albert Museum).

The breakfast room.

THE GREAT STAIRCASE

The staircase, begun by Chambers, is set behind a screen of Corinthian columns in which are suspended lanterns with oil lamps designed by Adam and illustrated in *The Works in Architecture of Robert and James Adam*, 1778. The stucco ceiling spandrels, designed by Adam in 1768, frame a giant octagon compartment incorporating a modern copy of Rubens's painting of George Villiers, first Duke of Buckingham (1592–1628), being escorted by Minerva and Mercury to the Temple of Virtus and being offered a garland by the three Graces, while Envy attempts to pull him down.

The original painting,[4] for which a sketch exists in the National Gallery, was commissioned in 1625 for York House, London. In 1697, a few years after the destruction of York House, it was purchased by Sir Francis Child in Amsterdam, and remained at the Childs' house in Lincoln's Inn Fields until Robert Child acquired a new London house in Berkeley Square in 1767. The Rubens was destroyed by fire, together with other large paintings from the gallery, while being transported to Jersey in 1949.

The great staircase.

The sketch of the *Apotheosis of the Duke of Buckingham* by Rubens (1577–1640), reproduced by courtesy of the Trustees, The National Gallery, London.

The great staircase.

THE YELLOW TAFFETA BEDCHAMBER

This is the principal guest bedroom and it is decorated en suite with a dressing room, which can be reached by a concealed door to the right of the bed. Chambers designed the room in the late 1750s, with an elegant plaster frieze of scrolling acanthus foliage, and a wooden chimneypiece, which is inset with *verde antico* marble. The chimneypiece frieze is carved with a Grecian anthemion and scrolling foliage, and is supported by scroll trusses ornamented with laurel garlands, vases of foliage, and draped female masks. The frames of the pier glass and matching overmantel glass, which incorporates a Chinese landscape painted mirror, are carved with foliage, palmettes and scallop shells, garlanded with laurel and suspended from bowed ribbons.

The satinwood bed, inlaid with green stained wood and carved with gilt enrichments, was designed by Adam in 1779, and supplied by Linnell. The foliate frieze of the cornice is surmounted by cupped acorns, while garlanded tablets support cupids holding laurel-wreathed vases. The bed is hung in Chinese yellow taffeta which is painted with flowers and foliage, bordered with green silk and lined with white silk. The window curtains and the squab cushions of the cane seated chairs are en suite. The Indian embroidered cotton counterpane for the bed, and the Brussels bedside carpet, no longer survive. The satinwood chairs are painted with green ornament and their splats are formed as Cupid's quiver-of-arrows. The satinwood bow-fronted chest of drawers and tambour-fronted night-tables are inlaid to correspond with the bed, and in addition there is a satinwood pembroke table. The wall-hangings are modern and the eighteenth-century chimney-board, covered with Chinese wallpaper, has been brought here from another room. Many rooms on this floor were hung with Chinese floral wallpaper and, together with the profusion of lacquer chests and oriental porcelain, caused one contemporary visitor to exclaim that she could almost fancy herself in Peking.

LEFT: The yellow taffeta bedchamber.

OVERLEAF: Chinese landscape painted mirror and the satinwood bed.

MR CHILD'S DRESSING ROOM

This is the first room of the Childs' apartment and has a door communicating with their bedroom. Its cornice and chimneypiece, ornamented with foliage bound by ribbons, are designed by Chambers, although the architrave of the doors would appear to survive from the Osterley of the late seventeenth century. The room was recently painted to match Mrs Child's dressing room, and the curtains, which were copied from those in the adjoining bedroom, replace the 'blue lustring festoon window curtains' listed in the 1782 inventory. None of Mr Child's dressing room furniture survives at Osterley, and his mahogany wardrobe, fitted with drawers and wire-panelled doors lined with silk, has been replaced by a mid eighteenth-century painted bookcase; his mahogany chairs by painted 'rout' chairs; his mahogany shaving-stand by a mid eighteenth-century reading table; his painted oval pier glass by a mid eighteenth-century mirror bearing the Child family crest; and his mahogany commode with fitted dressing drawer by one lent from the Victoria and Albert Museum. The built-in cupboard dates from the late nineteenth century.

LEFT: Indian embroided hangings. RIGHT: Chinese lacquer dressing table.

MR AND MRS CHILD'S BEDCHAMBER

The chimneypiece is en suite with that in the adjoining dressing room. The bed has mahogany posts, and 'sweep' cornices, which are upholstered to match the original floral embroidered cotton hangings, imported from Dacca by the East India Company. Only the dark stained valances survive and, like the festoon window curtains, are lined with green silk, and date from around 1765. The matching chair cover is one of a set of six, which originally fitted mahogany chairs (now missing).

The seventeenth-century French ebony cabinet and the Chinese lacquer dressing table furnished the room in the 1760s, but the Childs' original pier glass has been replaced by a gold painted one; their mahogany night table and pot cupboard have been replaced by the bedsteps, which were supplied for the state bedchamber in the 1880s, and their Wilton bedside carpet by a modern one.

MRS CHILD'S DRESSING ROOM

Chambers designed the cornice, with its acanthus-entwined rosettes, and the doors and window shutters, with their octagon panels. The acanthus scroll chimneypiece and overmantel mirror, which incorporates Francis Cotes's crayon portrait of Robert Child's daughter Sarah Anne (1763–1793), were designed and executed by Linnell about 1765. The mantelpiece is painted white to correspond with the marble inset, and the gilt oval mirror, with palm frond frame and glass borders, incorporates brackets for vases and is surmounted by a basket of flowers. Linnell also supplied a pair of gilt pier glasses and floral inlaid commodes, which now belong to Lord Jersey. The gilt pelmets may have been moved here from the drawing room when it was modernised in the 1770s. Mrs Child's 'blue lustring festoon window curtains' have been replaced by modern copies, and the wall-paper has been painted to match traces of blue paint found behind the mantelpiece. A gilt wood cabinet, designed by Adam to display Mrs Child's collection of gold filigree, no longer survives. Nor does her lacquer-panelled secretaire, nor her dressing table with its white quilted coat covered with Indian gold-worked muslin and its gilt looking-glass with matching 'veil'. The seventeenth-century Japanese lacquer cabinet supported on an early eighteenth-century stand is the only item of furniture surviving from the 1770s, when Walpole described the room as being full of 'pictures, gold filigree, china and japan'.

RIGHT: Mrs Child's dressing room. OVERLEAF: Sarah Anne Child by Francis Cotes (1726–70).

THE DRAWING ROOM

The ceiling plasterwork with octagon compartments framing an elliptical rosette is inspired by Robert Wood's engraving of the soffit of the Temple of the Sun at Palmyra. It is thought to have been designed by William Chambers in the late 1750s, and the seat furniture, attributed to John Linnell, is likely to have been supplied about 1760. The ceiling, which may originally have been painted white and gold, was picked out in colours when Adam remodelled the room in 1772, and hung the walls in 'pea green' damask. He also inserted a new frieze with Grecian anthemion and a chimneypiece with sphinxes supporting a vase of flowers on its central tablet. The overdoor tablets, with medallions supported by griffins, were carved to correspond with the chimneypiece and painted to match the ceiling. The floral 'mosaic' carpet was designed by Adam in 1774 to echo the ceiling, and was supplied by Thomas Moore (*c.* 1700–88), of Moorfields. Adam's designs of the previous year for the pier-glasses surmounted by sphinxes and for the elliptical 'Etruscan' commodes were also influenced by the architectural ornament of the room. The frames of the ormolu-mounted marquetry commode-tables, which are hollow inside, are ornamented with oval medallions of bacchantes or festive female figures, which are partly inspired by engravings of antique gems and the paintings discovered at Herculaneum. The circular medallions are taken from engravings after paintings by Angelica Kauffmann (1741–1807), symbolising sacred and profane love, with the chaste huntress Diana on one and 'Venus explaining to Cupid the torch of Hymen' on the other. The commodes are attributed to the firm of William Ince and John Mayhew, and the marquetry medallions to the Swedish cabinet-maker and specialist 'inlayer' Christopher Fuhrlohg. Love-birds appear on the Indian embroidered panel of the fire-screen, and glass ostrich eggs, mounted as ormolu candelabra by Matthew Boulton, are placed on tripod candlestands in the corners of the room. The stands are carved with rams' heads, to match those on the chimneypiece and doors. The gold coloured grate and fender, designed by Adam, are made of paktong, an alloy of zinc, copper and nickel.

The drawing room ceiling.

THE ANTECHAMBER *(Tapestry Room)*

The antechamber is the first of the three rooms in the State Apartment whose ceilings were designed by Adam in 1772 with low relief plasterwork picked out in a variety of colours and inset with decorative painted medallions. This combination of 'grotesque' plasterwork combined with cameo-like paintings was partly inspired by the ornament of Roman baths and villas, such as appeared in Charles Cameron, *The Baths of the Romans*, 1772, and partly by Renaissance ornament, such as Adam had studied in the Villa Madama, Rome. The inset medallion of the antechamber ceiling is taken from the frontispiece of Antonio Gori's *Museum Florentinum*, 1732, and depicts 'The Dedication of a Child to Minerva', which was no doubt an appropriate pun on the family name of Child. Female figures representing the Liberal Arts appear in the corner medallions and are garlanded with flowers.

The French Gobelins tapestries were ordered in 1772, shortly after the arrival in London of a related set belonging to George Williams, sixth Earl of Coventry. The overmantel is signed by Jacques Neilson, the Scottish Director of the Gobelins, and bears the date 1775. Tapestries of this design, representing the Elements, as personified by The Loves of the Gods, had originally been commissioned in the 1760s by Madame de Pompadour's brother, the Marquis de Marigny, who was *Directeur et Ordonnateur des Bâtiments, Jardins etc.* to Louis XV. They were conceived by the neo-classical architect Jacques Germain Soufflot and are woven with *trompe l'œil* medallion paintings by François Boucher, who held the post of *Inspecteur* at the Gobelins, and are ornamented with flowers designed by Maurice Jacques and Louis Tessier. The medallion of 'Fire', represented by Venus visiting Vulcan in his forge, hangs opposite the fireplace, and those facing the windows are 'Air', represented by Aurora, the Dawn Goddess discovering the hunter Cephalus, and 'Earth', represented by Pomona, the goddess of gardens and orchards, being wooed by Vertumnus, god of Spring, who, according to the story in Ovid's *Metamorphoses*, assumed the disguise of an old lady in order to sing his own praises. In place of 'Water' a mirror is hung between the windows. The overmantel of Cupid and Psyche was inspired by Apuleius's romance of the second century, *The Golden Ass*. The story proved a popular subject for the decoration of bedrooms and boudoirs, and the scene depicted here shows

LEFT:
The antechamber ceiling.

OVERLEAF:
The antechamber.

Psyche about to wake Cupid by spilling oil from her lamp on to his wing. The young Cupid, in the medallion to the left of the fireplace, uses the sun's rays to light his torch, while the medallion cut from the tapestry in the window pier and used to make a fire-screen (not exhibited) shows Cupid using the torch to heat his arrows of love. The pink foliage on the 'claret' ground of the tapestries creates the effect of a bower, ornamented for a festival with garlands and vases of flowers, and in which birds and animals appear together with trophies of sport and love. Cupids above the sofa bear a thyrsus and rose-entwined stick,

PREVIOUS PAGES: *Pomona being wooed by Vertumnus* and *Cupid and Psyche.*

LEFT: The garden maid chair back.

RIGHT: The Gobelins antechamber.

while on the back of the sofa a shepherd woos a shepherdess. A young gardener on one chair doffs his cap at the adjoining seat, where a garden maid leans coyly on her rake. The tapestry chair backs, representing the seasons, portray scenes from Boucher's *Les Amours Pastorales*, while their seats are strewn with flowers. The chair frames were designed by Linnell in the French *goût grec* style to correspond with the tapestry ornament. Great baskets of flowers and fruit appear on the carpet, woven by Moore, and female figures and cupids garland vases and a tazza of flowers on the crest of the pier glass, which was designed by Adam in 1775.

Medallions of Venus and Cupid, Cupid astride a dolphin (an attribute of Venus) and Cupid astride a lion (symbolising Love conquering Strength) appear on the chimneypiece, which is inset with scagliola plaques in imitation of Florentine hardstone mosaic. A corresponding scagliola slab between the windows is supported on a gilt frame, which is decorated with painted medallions of Erato, Muse of love poetry, together with cupids. Festive female figures appear on the tripod stands, which support ormolu mounted bluejohn and glass candelabra.

ABOVE: Love trophy on the
west wall.

RIGHT: The tapestry room.

THE STATE BEDCHAMBER

The green painted ceiling is inset with a central medallion, inspired by Angelica Kauffmann's painting of the Grace, Aglaia, who was a nature goddess and one of Venus's attendants, being enslaved by Love. The other paintings, including one depicting the shepherd extolling to Erminia the pleasures of the pastoral life, are inspired by subjects described in Torquato Tasso, *The Recovery of Jerusalem*.

The architecture of the eight-poster bed was inspired by Robert Wood's engraving of the Temple of the Sun, published in his *Ruins of Baalbek*, 1757, and by details taken from Grecian temples published in Stuart's *Antiquities of Athens*. It was designed by Adam in 1775–76 and conceived as a Temple of Venus, such as appeared in contemporary gardens which were modelled on the theme of Arcadia (the ideal region of rural happiness). Its headboard is carved with nymphs garlanding a medallion of Venus, the goddess of love and fertility, together with her attributes of cupids astride dolphins. The hangings are of green velvet and silk embroidered with flowers in coloured silks while the valances are embroidered in gilt thread with poppy heads, emblem of sleep, alternating with the Child 'eagle' crest. The domed canopy is garlanded with silk flowers and perched at the corners are sphinxes (the protectors of the garden of Arcadia).[5] Addorsed sphinxes support the 'medallion' backs of the chairs as well as the medallion, painted with Venus and cupid, on the crest of the pier glass. The mantelpiece is embellished with cupids' attributes, while cupids are carved on the crest of the overmantel mirror and support a painted medallion, surmounted by the Child crest. The floral bedside carpet designed by Adam in 1778 was supplied by Thomas Moore, and the neo-classical commode, constructed from panels of a Chinese lacquer screen, is attributed to Thomas Chippendale (1718–79). The original velvet wall-hangings were replaced with silk in the 1880s and this was renewed in the 1950s. The entwined poppies carved on the window embrasure are inspired by pilaster ornament engraved in Wood's *Ruins of Baalbek*.

The painted medallion on the ceiling.

TOP: The headboard.

BOTTOM: Detail of valances with the Child's family crest.

RIGHT: The state bed.

OVERLEAF: The state bedchamber, the sphinx-support detail on the chair and the chair.

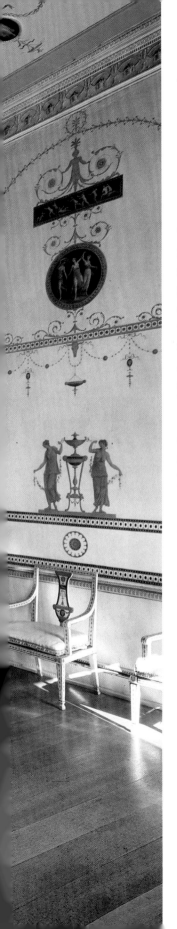

THE ETRUSCAN DRESSING ROOM

The dressing room is papered and painted by Adam's decorative artist Pietro Mario Borgnis (1743–1801), to resemble an open loggia with 'Etruscan' terracotta and black arabesque trellis-work on a sky-blue ground. The Italian architect Giovanni Battista Piranesi (1720–78), in *Diverse Maniere D'adornare I Cammini*, 1769, had proposed the imitation of the Etruscan style by decorating walls with ornament inspired by ancient urns, bas reliefs, etc. However, this novel form of decoration, reflecting the influence of engravings of the Domus Aurea in Rome as well as being inspired by Italian Renaissance 'grotesque' decoration and the ornament and colouring of 'Etruscan' vases, was claimed by the Adam brothers in the preface to their *Works in Architecture*, Vol. II, 1778, to have first been introduced by them at the Countess of Derby's dressing room in Grosvenor Square. They also stated that Mr Child had been amongst the 'many persons of rank and fortune' who had been 'struck and pleased with the taste'.

In the 1760s an attempt was made to promote 'Etruscan' culture as the font and origin of the whole of classical antiquity. The interest in Attic red-figure vases was boosted by Sir William Hamilton's sponsorship of the French scholar, Pierre François d'Hancarville's *Catalogue of Etruscan, Greek and Roman Antiquities*, 1766–67, and his gift to the British Museum in 1772 of the vases which he had acquired while British Ambassador at the Court of Naples. In addition, the fashion for these vases had been fostered by the 'basalt' replicas sold in the London showrooms of Josiah Wedgwood and Thomas Bentley, which had opened in 1769. They also sold black 'basalt' tablets, medallions and cameos, which they described in their catalogue as being suitable for 'inlaying in the panels of rooms . . . or as pictures in dressing rooms'.

Etruria in central Italy was said to have been founded after the Trojan wars, and this inspired the scene in the dressing room ceiling medallion, which shows Hector departing for the Trojan wars and bidding farewell to Andromache. Homer's description of her devotion to her husband's memory, following his death in battle, was one of the epic love stories which was particularly popular in the late eighteenth century. Oval medallions of festive

The Etruscan dressing room.

OPPOSITE TOP:
The ceiling.

OPPOSITE BOTTOM: The
wall of the Etruscan dressing
room.

ABOVE: 'Etruscan' vase on
the mantelpiece.

female figures are suspended between plaster tripods on the ceiling, and also appear in the corners of the walls, for which Adam provided designs in 1773. The walls are decorated like a neo-classical printroom, and painted with maidens dancing round tripods. These are framed within arabesque arches from which are suspended colourful medallions and tablets of nymphs and sporting children celebrating rites of love at the Feast of Venus, as described by Ovid. Baskets of apples, an attribute of Venus, are suspended along the plaster frieze, and the mantelpiece is carved with gem-like figures of Cupid bearing a rose, another attribute of Venus, and Cupid with his burning torch, an attribute of Love. A *trompe l'œil* garniture of vases and female figures with a tazza of flowers is painted above the chimneypiece, which is fitted with a canvas chimney-board, ornamented with arabesques and a sacrificial scene. The pier glass, above the lacquer mounted commode, is inset with a painted medallion of 'Love nurtured by Hope', and carved with female figures with vases and a basket of flowers.

The east wall.

LEFT: Medallion above the
mantelpiece.

RIGHT: The pier glass and
commode.

The cane-seated chairs were designed by Adam in 1776 and painted to correspond with the ornament of the furniture in the window piers. Their squab cushions are upholstered in French grey silk (modern), matching the festoon window curtains with their 'Etruscan' coloured fringes (original). The thyrsus-pole firescreen bears a floral embroidered panel, designed by Adam and worked by Mrs Child in 1777. The pembroke table is decorated by Henry Clay of Covent Garden with a 'Scene in the Garden of the Hesperides' painted from d'Hancarville's engraving of one of William Hamilton's finest vases. The room would also have been filled with vases and pots of flowers; indeed 'The Garden of Love' is the unifying theme between the apparently disparate decorations of the state apartment with its 'French' antechamber, 'English' bedroom and 'Italian' dressing room.

ABOVE: The pembroke table and painted chairs.

RIGHT: The festoon window curtain with 'Etruscan' coloured fringes.

EARLY HISTORY

Sir Thomas Gresham's Osterley.

Osterley or Oysterley

'*The house nowe of the ladie Gresham's, a faire and stately building of bricke, erected by Sir Thomas Gresham, Knight, Citizen and Marchant-Adventurer of London, and finished about anno 1577. It standeth in a parke by him also impaled, well-wooded, and garnished with manie faire ponds, which afforde not only fish and fowle, as swanes, and other water fowle; but also great use for milles, as paper milles, oyle milles, and corne milles, all of which are now decayed (a corne mill excepted). In the same parke was a very faire Heronrie, for the increase and preservation whereof, sundrie allurements were devised and set up, fallen all to ruin.*'

This passage from John Norden's *Speculum Britanniae*, published in 1596, is the earliest account of a house at Osterley. Sir Thomas Gresham (1519?–79), perhaps the richest English merchant of his age, the founder of the Royal Exchange and of Gresham's College, had bought the manor in 1562 and must have started building soon afterwards. The site was apparently not that of the old manorial dwelling, but according to Norden (in his manuscript additions to his book) that of a farm, 'purchased by the sayd Sir Thomas, graced now with a house beseeming a prince'. The new house was ready to live in by 1576, when Queen Elizabeth stayed there, as we learn from an indictment in the Gaol Delivery Rolls of that year against two women who, while the Queen was in residence, 'maliciously, diabolically and illegally' tore up the palings round the park 'to the great disquiet and disturbance of the said lady the Queen.'[6] Thomas Fuller also records her visit to Osterley in his *Worthies*, 1661, and relates that 'her Majesty found fault with the court of this house as too great; affirming that "it would appear more handsome, if divided with a wall in the middle." What doth Sir Thomas, but in the night-time sends for workmen to London (money commands all things), who so speedily and silently apply their business, that the next morning discovered that court double, which the night had left single before. It is questionable whether the Queen next day was more contented with the conformity to her fancy, or more pleased with the surprise and sudden performance thereof; whilst her courtiers disported themselves with their several expressions, some affirming it was no wonder he could so soon *change* a building, who could build a '*Change*; others (reflecting on some known differences in this Knight's family) affirmed that "any house is easier divided than united".'

Sir Thomas's Gresham's 'faire and stately' building with its four corner towers still stands, though enlarged and completely encased in new walls in the eighteenth century. Recent investigations of wall and roof construction suggest that the Elizabethan house was only one room deep throughout and that the area now occupied by the Hall and North and South Passages was part of the original courtyard. The arrangement of chimney-stacks and sections of old wall indicate that there were small turrets or extruded corners at the angles of the courtyard, the one in the north-west corner apparently having contained a spiral staircase.

A more surprising discovery is that the vaulting under the courtyard is early – possibly Elizabethan – implying that the raised courtyard was a feature of the original house and not introduced by Adam, as has hitherto been supposed. Such a feature, though not unknown, was very unusual at that time. (A notable example was at Wimbledon House, built in 1588, but in that instance it was probably suggested by the sloping site.) A representation of Osterley on a map drawn by Moses Glover in 1638[7] (see page 9) appears to show a block containing an entrance gateway enclosing the fourth side of the inner courtyard; in front can be seen a large forecourt of the usual Elizabethan type but with the additional feature of a wall dividing it across the middle – presumably the one that Queen Elizabeth caused to be built.

Seventeenth-century Osterley

After Gresham's death in 1579 the property was neglected, as we learn from Norden. His widow bequeathed it to Sir William Read, her son by her first husband. After his death in 1621 it passed through the hands of several different owners, among them Sir Edward Coke (1552–1634), afterwards Lord Chief Justice, George, Earl of Desmond, and Sir William Waller, the Parliamentary general, who died at Osterley in 1668. In 1683 it was bought by Nicholas Barbon (d. 1698), a builder and speculator who erected many buildings in London after the Great Fire and instituted fire insurance in England.

THE CHILD FAMILY

The transformation of the house to its present-day appearance would not have happened but for a certain Francis Child, the fifth son of an obscure clothier of Headington in Wiltshire who, starting from next to nothing, amassed a fortune that placed it in his descendants' power to transform and eclipse their predecessors' work.

Born in 1642, he was sent young to try his luck in London and became apprenticed, at the age of fourteen, to a goldsmith named William Hall. Afterwards he entered the firm of another goldsmith, William Wheeler, in whose shop love and fortune soon favoured him, as we may gather from a marriage licence dated 2 October 1671, which reads: 'Francis Child, of St Clement Danes, citizen, goldsmith, bachelor, about 28, and Mistress Elizabeth Wheeler, of same, spinster, about 19, consent of mother, Mrs Martha Blanchard, alias Wheeler.' The bride's mother, here mentioned, having lost her first husband William Wheeler in 1663, had married Robert Blanchard and made over to him the management of the business. Child's marriage with Elizabeth Wheeler gave him a family interest in a flourishing concern. By 1677 he was a partner in the firm of 'Blanchard and Child at the Marygold', as it is entitled in the *Little London Directory* that year. At Blanchard's death four years afterwards Child became head of the firm and inherited both the Wheeler and Blanchard fortunes.

Meantime, several London goldsmiths, Child among them, had been going in more and more for a profitable sideline, that of banking or looking after other people's money. So the modern English banks grew up, and a number of goldsmiths eventually abandoned their original trade altogether and applied themselves exclusively to banking. Child is reputed to have been the first to take this step and for that reason has been called 'the father of the profession'. His bank, after a flourishing existence of two hundred years, was merged with Messrs Glyn Mills (now Williams and Glyn's Bank plc), but a branch known as 'Child's Bank' still carries on business on the original premises at no. 1 Fleet Street, 'at the sign of the Marygold', as it was called in the days before houses were given numbers, when every tradesman hung a sign above his door. These signs were often taken over from a previous owner; and the Marygold had been the sign of a tavern.

Robert Child, Mrs Robert Child (Sarah Jodrell) and Sarah Anne Child in 1781; crayon by Margaret Battine after Daniel Gardner from the collection of the Earl of Jersey.

Through his wealth, ability and public spirit, Francis Child rose to a prominent position in the City, being knighted in 1689 and elected Lord Mayor in 1698. He was also a Member of Parliament during most of Queen Anne's reign, sitting at different times for Devizes and the City. In 1711 he enters our story by buying the Osterley estate from the executors of Dr Nicholas Barbon. He apparently never lived there, preferring East End House, the residence he built for himself at Parson's Green on a site inherited from his partner Robert Blanchard.

Sir Francis, who was the model for William Hogarth's 'Industrious Apprentice', died at Parsons Green in 1713. Of his twelve sons only four survived him, three of them succeeding to Osterley: Robert, the eldest (1674–1721), Francis, the seventh (1684–1740) and Samuel, the youngest (1693–1752). All three of them carried on the family business, played an active part in City affairs and sat in Parliament, Robert and Francis each earning a knighthood and dying unmarried. Samuel was succeeded by his son, Francis (1735–63), who initiated the great building operations that transformed the Tudor house to its present appearance. But Francis did not live to see the completion of his plans for he died in 1763 on the point of marrying. Horace Walpole, his neighbour at Twickenham, who took a lively interest in the house and family, was shocked at the sudden reversal of fortune, but he added that 'the young lover died handsomely, £50,000 will dry tears that at the most could be but two months old . . . here is a charming wife for anybody that likes a sentimental situation, a pretty woman and a large fortune.'[8] His younger brother Robert (1739–82) completed the reconstruction of the house; but he too died prematurely, at the age of forty-three, his end being hastened, it was said, by grief at the undutiful behaviour of his only child, Sarah Anne.

This high-spirited girl fell in love at the age of eighteen with John Fane, tenth Earl of Westmorland, a young man of twenty-two, who soon proved that he deserved his nickname 'Rapid Westmorland'. For knowing that her father had other ideas for Sarah Anne, he asked him one evening at dinner, 'Child, suppose that you were in love with a girl, and her father refused his consent to the union, what should *you* do?' 'Why! run away with her, to be sure!' the banker rashly replied. The young man took his advice, and in the small hours of Friday morning, 17 May 1782, Sarah Anne stole away from her father's house, no. 38 Berkeley Square, and was soon with her lover in a post-chaise, bound for Gretna Green. It was not long before her flight was discovered, and Mr and Mrs Child set out in pursuit, sending two men ahead on swift horses with orders to arrest the fleeing couple. As the horsemen drew level with his carriage, the Earl aimed his pistol at them, but hesitated to fire. 'Shoot, my Lord!' cried Sarah Anne, and the next moment one of Mr Child's favourite

Lady Ducie (Mrs Robert Child) and her daughter Lady Westmorland, crayon by John Russell from the collection of the Earl of Jersey.

hunters lay dead under his groom. The parents meantime were delayed by a stratagem of the Earl's. Passing a detachment of the King's Dragoon Guards exercising on the road to the North, he had recognised the commander as an old friend and had begged him to slow down the pursuit. When the Childs came up they found the road obstructed by troops and were forced to wait until the manoeuvre was completed. Soon after Baldock they gave up and turned back, while the lovers sped on their way and were married in an alehouse at Gretna Green the next day. It was not long before they were forgiven and married over again more regularly. Mrs Child administered the mildest rebuke to her daughter. 'My dear,' she said, 'why were you so hasty, when I had much better parties in view for you?' 'Mamma,' Lady Westmorland replied, 'a bird in the hand is worth two in the bush.'[9] Mr Child's disappointment was more effectively expressed in the new will he made just before his death two months after the elopement; for he bequeathed Osterley and the bulk of his great fortune to the *second* son of Sarah Anne's future children, or, failing such a son, to the eldest daughter, no doubt in the hope of ensuring that the elder branch of the Westmorland family should draw no great financial advantage from the runaway match. Osterley thus passed to Sarah Sophia Fane, Lady Westmorland's second child.

FRANCIS CHILD AND WILLIAM CHAMBERS

Francis Child came of age in 1756, and started in earnest to transform the old mansion at Osterley, which he had inherited four years previously, into a Palladian villa set in a landscaped park. While there is no documentary evidence there are nonetheless strong stylistic reasons supporting the family tradition that the Scottish architect William Chambers (1723–96) was consulted at this stage. Shortly after returning in 1755 from his architectural studies in Italy, Chambers was appointed architectural tutor to the Prince of Wales, afterwards King George III, and architect in charge of Princess Augusta's pleasure gardens at Kew – the planning of parks and gardens then being an important part of the architect's profession.

At Osterley Child and Chambers created the series of serpentine lakes, which sweep past the house like a tributary of the Thames, and which in the eighteenth century supported a variety of pleasure boats including a Chinese sampan. Combined with his knowledge of classical architecture, Chambers was also a leading authority on Chinese architecture and gardens, and built a Chinese tea-house (no longer extant), which may have been situated on the island at the head of the lakes. On the west side of the house Chambers laid out the 'arcadian' pleasure garden with its Doric Temple of Pan. He also remodelled the stable block and, with Boulton Mainwaring as his executant architect, began the transformation of the great house. He rebuilt the west front with its central pediment and decorated various rooms in the classical style. The principal ones were fitted with marble chimneypieces, supplied by the sculptor Joseph Wilton, who had accompanied him back from Italy.

FRANCIS CHILD AND ROBERT ADAM

Like many other patrons of his day, who gathered ideas from a number of architects, Child also consulted the Scottish architect Robert Adam (1728–92), who had recently established his architectural practice in Grosvenor Street. During his four years in Italy (1754–58), Adam had learnt from the Italian artist/architect Giovanni Battista Piranesi, and from the French artist Charles Louis Clérisseau, a picturesque neo-classical approach to the 'antique', which combined intellectual and stylistic freedom. His revolutionary new designs had an immediate success in London, and in 1761, the year that he became Architect to King George III's Office of Works (a post which he shared with Chambers), he was employed to provide designs for completing the villa and park at Osterley.

ROBERT CHILD AND ROBERT ADAM

After Francis Child's death in 1763, his brother Robert Child amended and carried forward Adam's building schemes. His designs, dating from 1766, for completing and altering the interior decoration contain features whose origins can be traced to other houses in which he was involved such as Kedleston Hall, Derbyshire, Croome Court, Worcestershire, Nostell Priory, Yorkshire, and Syon House, Middlesex. Likewise his designs dating from 1772 for the decoration and furnishing of the small scale rooms in the state apartment interweave with his designs for other London houses.

The 'revolutionary' change that they had brought about in interior decoration, during the twenty years since William Chambers published his *Treatise on Civil Architecture*, 1758, was noted by Robert and James Adam in the preface to their *Works in Architecture*, 1773: 'The massive entablature, the ponderous compartment ceiling, the tabernacle frame, almost the only species of ornament formerly known, in this country, are now universally exploded, and in their place, we have adopted a beautiful variety of light mouldings, gracefully formed, delicately enriched and arranged with propriety and skill. We have introduced a great variety of ceilings, friezes, and decorated pilasters and have added grace and beauty to the whole by a mixture of grotesque stucco and painted ornament together with the flowing rainceau, with its fanciful figures and winding foliage ... we flatter ourselves, we have been able to sieze, with some degree of success, the beautiful spirit of antiquity, and to transfuse it, with novelty and variety.' *The Works*, 1773–78, which illustrates the Adam brothers' unified yet varied dictionary of forms had been issued in parts since 1773, and included a number of designs for furnishings which had been executed for Osterley in the 1760s, but appear to have been originally drawn up for Syon House.

One client described Adam arriving at her door with a whole regiment of 'artificers', and it was this team of artists, draughtsmen and craftsmen that enabled the Adam firm to produce its remarkably unified decorative schemes, where everything from the ceiling to the door escutcheon came within the realm of the architect. The majority of Adam's designs for Osterley are preserved at the Sir John Soane's Museum, although a few remain at the house itself.

A visitor to Osterley in the eighteenth century commented that she did not know if Mr Child was a man of 'Taste', but thought that he had at least shown his 'Good sense in permitting his house to be decorated by those who indisputedly profess the most refined ideas of it'. However Robert Child was clearly a cognoscente of neo-classicism, owned a fine library, subscribed to contemporary publications on classical architecture, consulted the leading scholars of the day such as Dr Thomas Morell, collected coins and medals and was clearly as 'Antique Mad' as many of his contemporaries. He no doubt shared the views of another of Adam's important patrons, Sir Nathaniel Curzon (1726–1804), who wrote in his notebook concerning his house, Kedleston Hall, in Derbyshire,

> Grant me ye Gods, a pleasant seat
> In attick elegance made neat
> Fine lawns, much wood, and water plenty
> (Of deer, and herds not scanty)
> Laid out in such an uncurb'd taste
> That nature may'nt be lost but grac'd
> Within doors, rooms of fair extent
> Enriched with decent ornament
> Choice friends, rare books, sweet musick's strain
> But little business: and no pain
> Good meats, rich wines, that may give birth
> To free but not ungracious mirth
> A lovely mistress kind and fair
> whose gentle looks disperse all care.

Osterley in 1772

'Osterley (the Seat of Mr Child) is a square brick building with Towers at the 4 corners, it has the appearance of a Castle at a distance, three sides of it surround a Court, and the fourth which is to be the grand entrance is fill'd up with a collonade of stone, that is unusual and magnificent enough, it is not quite finish'd but there are already several very fine rooms; one enters, at present, at the rustick door and going up a staircase, we are led into a hall which I think rather too low but I am not sure, it is finely ornamented with stucco ornaments white and the ground a greenish light grey; out of this we go into the Gallery, which runs the whole length of the Garden front, it is hung with pea-green paper, and fill'd with a noble collection of pictures, there are four very large plates of glass in it, which Mr Child purchased at Gunnersbury, and are I think larger than those in his House in Town, out of this Gallery we are conducted into the drawing room which is a beautiful room, hung with pea-green damask, furniture the same, the ceiling is extremely elegant, painted & gilt, and the carpet, which is from Mr Moores manufactory answers to the ceiling; there are some fine pictures in this room also – on the other side of the Hall, is the

Eating room the Breakfast room, the Library, the first is a very large room, the ornaments of Stucco, white, upon different grounds, *Pantheon fashion*. The sideboard was magnificently furnished with plate, and under the Table was a Massy & large silver Cistern. The Tables between the windows were antique tesselated Tables from Italy, the Glasses very fine. The Breakfast room is Lemon colour, with blew ornaments, the Chairs Mrs Childs own work, in very elegant frames, in quite a new taste, the walls are hung full of pictures, and the beautiful portrait of Mrs Child, by Cotes is over the Chimney. The Library is a charming room, It is fill'd with fine Books, and Mr Adams has lavished all his taste in ornamenting every part. it is plain white the Tables, Desks, & chairs are all of the fine inlaid work of different woods, and you cannot imagine how very elegant they are, and must have cost a great deal of money, but indeed one sees that no expence has been spared anywhere, The lodging rooms are in the atticks, and a great many there are, all the rooms have dressing rooms to them, and are furnished with the finest Chintzes, painted Taffatys, India paper & decker work, and such a profusion of rich China & Japan, that I could almost fancy myself in Peking. The Garden is laid out in the usual manner of Lawn

Two views in Osterley Park with exotic birds from the menagerie, crayon and watercolour (1757) by Anthony Devis (1729–1816) from a private collection.

shrubbery, and gravel walk, the park is very fine considering it is flat, and there is a large piece of water in it, one part much like the lake at Lord Leicester's with fine oaks washing their branches in its water: and a delightful shady walk along its banks. But the Menagerie is the prettiest place I ever saw, 'tis an absolute retreat, & fill'd with all sorts of curious and scarce Birds and Fowles, among the rest 2 numidian Cranes that follow like Dogs, and a pair of Chinese teal that have only been seen in England before upon the India paper, on the Lake there is a Scampan brought from China, it is a very large Vessel, there are several other pleasure boats besides.

Extract of a letter written in 1772 by Lady Beauchamp Proctor. In the possession of Mr G Yorke of Forthampton Court, Gloucester.

Osterley in 1773

An amusing description of the house is supplied by Horace Walpole (1717–97) who lived nearby at Strawberry Hill, a gothic villa overlooking the Thames near Richmond. His first letter, written after a visit in 1773, sparkles with enthusiasm and wit.

'On Friday we went to see – oh! the palace of palaces! – and yet a palace sans crown, sans coronet, but such expense! such taste! such profusion! and yet half an acre produces all the rents that furnish such magnificence. It is a Jaghire got without a crime. In short, a shop is the estate, and Osterley Park is the spot. The old house I have often seen, which was built by Sir Thomas Gresham; but it is so improved and enriched, that all the Percies and Seymours of Sion must die of envy. There is a double portico that fills the space between the towers of the front, and is as noble as the Propyleum of Athens. There is a hall, library, breakfast-room, eating-room, all chef d'œuvre of Adam, a gallery one hundred and thirty feet long, and a drawing-room worthy of Eve before the Fall. Mrs Child's dressing-room is full of pictures, gold filigree, china and japan. So is all the house; the chairs are taken from antique lyres, and make charming harmony; there are Salvators, Gaspar Poussins, and in a beautiful staircase, a ceiling by Rubens. Not to mention a kitchen-garden that costs £1,400 a-year, a menagerie full of birds that come from a thousand islands, which Mr Banks has not yet discovered: and then, in the drawing-room I mentioned, there are door-cases, and a crimson and gold frieze, that I believe were borrowed from the Palace of the Sun; and then the Park is – the ugliest spot of ground in the universe – so I returned comforted to Strawberry.'

Horace Walpole to the Countess of Upper Ossory, 21 June 1773, *Letters*, ed. Mrs Paget Toynbee, Vol. VIII, 1904, pp. 291–2.

His second letter followed a visit to see the recently completed state apartment, and is written in a more waspish vein.

'Mr Nichols and I went last week to see the new apartment at Osterley Park. The first chamber, a drawing-room, not a large one, is the most superb and beautiful that can be imagined, and hung with gobelin tapestry, and enriched by Adam in his best taste, except that he has stuck diminutive heads in bronze, no bigger than a half-crown, into the chimney-piece's hair. The next is a light plain green velvet bedchamber. The bed is of green satin richly embroidered with colours, and with eight columns; too theatric, and too like a modern head-dress, for round the outside of the dome are festoons of artificial flowers. What would Vitruvius think of a dome decorated by a milliner? The last chamber after these two proud rooms, chills you: it is called the Etruscan, and is painted all over like Wedgwood's ware, with black and yellow small grotesques. Even the chairs are of painted wood. It would be a pretty waiting-room in a garden. I never saw such a profound tumble into the Bathos. It is going out of a palace into a potter's field. Tapestry, carpets, glass, velvet, satin, are all attributes of winter. There could be no excuse for such a cold termination, but its containing a cold bath next to the bed-chamber: – and it is called taste to join these incongruities! I hope I have put you into a passion.'

Horace Walpole to the Rev William Mason, 16 July 1778, *Letters*, ed. Mrs Paget Toynbee, Vol X, 1904, p. 282.

Osterley in 1786

Unfortunately, when Thomas Jefferson and John Adams visited Osterley on 20 April 1786, they were unable to view the house, because they had failed to acquire a ticket in advance, and Mrs Child had gone to the races at Newmarket. Adams noted in his diary that 'The Verdure is charming, the Music of the Birds pleasant.' However he also wrote 'The beauty, Convenience, and Utility of these Country Seats, are not enjoyed by the owners. They are mere Ostentations of Vanity. Races, Cocking, Gambling, draw away their attention.'

W H Adams, *Jefferson and the Arts*, 1976, p. 153.

Osterley in 1809

. . . they went to dinner and 'The drawing-room in which we were received, and in which they always sit, is 10 or 11 feet high, and I think much broader than the gallery at Althorp. It is 130 feet long, and yet by means of two large chimney pieces, and a profusion of sofas, chairs and tables of all sizes, a billiard table, books, pictures, and a pianoforte, it was as comfortable and as well filled as a small room would. All the rest of the house is of a piece with this room – immense, magnificent, and very comfortable . . .'

Mrs Hugh Wyndham, *Corr. of Sarah Lady Lyttleton*, 1912, p. 75.

Osterley Park in 1920

'As Sunday evening draws in, the peals of distant church bells are the only sounds which come to break the quiet of a home so near the town and yet, seemingly, so secluded from the world; then these cease, and the song of the nightingales alone disturbs the slumbers of Osterley Park.'

M F Jersey, *Osterley Park*, 1920, p. 30.

THE JERSEY FAMILY

After Robert Child's death in 1782, his widow Sarah (1741–93) married in 1791 the Right Honorable Francis, Lord Ducie. On her death in 1793 Osterley passed to her grand-daughter, Sarah Sophia Fane (1785–1867), since her mother, Sarah Anne, Lady Westmorland, died in the same year. In 1804, at the age of nineteen, Sarah Sophia married George Villiers (1773–1859), who succeeded the following year as fifth Earl of Jersey and later took the name of Child before that of Villiers. The Countess became a leading figure in London society and was popularly known as 'Queen Sarah'. It was said that she was 'a great social power and was one of the famous committee who decided upon the rights of admission to Almack's, for which more qualifications were needed than most people possess for admission to heaven'.[10] She outlived her husband and her eldest son, the sixth Earl, who died only six weeks after his father. Thus on her death in 1867, at the age of eighty-two, Osterley passed to her grandson, Victor Albert George Child-Villiers, the seventh Earl (1845–1915).

From 1870–83 the house was leased to Caroline, Duchess of Cleveland. Augustus Hare, who gives several anecdotes about her in *The Story of my Life*, says that 'the old Duchess, stumping about with her ebony stick, seemed part of the place'.

After her death in 1883 the Earl and Countess of Jersey took up residence again and from then until the outbreak of the First World War Osterley was noted for its week-end house-parties, which were largely attended by prominent Conservative politicians and by writers.

On the death of his father in 1915, the eighth Earl inherited Osterley. He died in 1923 and it was his son, the ninth and present Earl, who gave the house and grounds to the nation.

Transport

Underground to Osterley Station (Piccadilly line); buses nos. 91 and 116; Green Line coach no. 704. After alighting from train or bus at Osterley Station, which is on the Great West Road, turn north up Thornbury Road (traffic lights) and enter Osterley Park by the gate in Jersey Road. A car park is available inside the grounds.

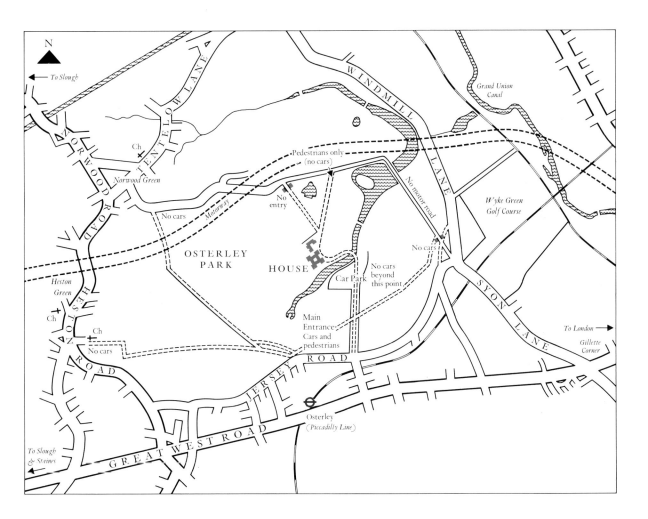

Book List

M F Jersey, *Osterley Park*, 1920.

The Earl of Jersey, *Osterley Park, Isleworth*, 1939.

Peter Ward-Jackson, *Osterley Park*, 1953.

P Thornton, *Osterley Park*, 1972, 2nd ed. 1977.

Notes

1. A catalogue of the 'Scarce and Valuable Stove, Green House and Hardy Plants' was made in 1794, and published by J Hardy, 'Osterley Park House: A Temple of Flora', *V & A Album*, vol. III, 1984, pp. 150–59.

2. In 1794 William Hayes, artist and ornithologist of Southall, Middlesex, published two illustrated volumes on the rare species of birds in this famous aviary.

3. The furniture at Osterley in detail is described in Maurice Tomlin's *Catalogue of Adam Period Furniture*, 1972, revised ed. 1981.

4. In the 1780s it was wrongly described as 'The Apotheosis of William Prince of Orange'.

5. The missing curtains and garlands were replaced in 1982 through the generosity of Williams and Glyn's Bank.

6. Middlesex County Record Office, Sessions Roll no. 199/4.

7. In the collection of His Grace the Duke of Northumberland at Syon House.

8. Walpole to George Montagu, 3 October 1763.

9. The story of the elopement is related at length by W A Thorpe in an article entitled 'Imperial Osterley' in *Connoisseur*, June and September, 1947.

10. E Balch, *Glimpses of Old English Houses*, 1890.

APSLEY HOUSE

THE WELLINGTON MUSEUM

149 Piccadilly, London W1
Telephone 01-499 5676

HAM HOUSE

near Richmond, Surrey
Telephone 01-940 1950

Apsley House, sometimes called 'Number One, London' was the home of the first Duke of Wellington, famous for his success in the Peninsula War, and later a leading statesman. He acquired the house from his brother Marquis Wellesley in 1817 and in the late 1820s employed Benjamin Dean Wyatt to create the present house, which encases the original brick house built by Robert Adam in the 1770s. The Duke's magnificent picture gallery contains paintings from the Spanish royal collection and among the many masterpieces displayed at the house are the Portuguese centrepiece and the Waterloo shield which commemorates his success at the Battle of Waterloo, 1815.

Open all year, Tuesday, Wednesday, Thursday and Saturday: 10.00 to 18.00. Sunday: 14.30 to 18.00.
Closed Good Friday, May Day Bank Holiday, Christmas Eve, Christmas Day, Boxing Day and New Year's Day.

There are regular guided tours, usually on Thursday at 13.00. Details of these and other talks can be obtained from the programmes issued by the Education Department, Victoria and Albert Museum, South Kensington, London SW7 2RL. Telephone: 01-589 6371, ext. 316 or 258.
Groups can obtain the services of a qualified guide lecturer through the Education Department, Victoria and Albert Museum as above.

Property of the National Trust;
administered by the Victoria and Albert Museum.

Originally built in 1610 by Sir Thomas Vavasour as a modest country residence, Ham House was enlarged and modernised by the Duke and Duchess of Lauderdale in the 1670s and contains most of the paintings and furniture from the period.

Open all year, Tuesday to Sunday inclusive, 11.00 to 17.00.
Closed Good Friday, May Day Bank Holiday, Christmas Eve, Christmas Day, Boxing Day and New Year's Day.

Guided tours can be arranged through the Education Department, Victoria and Albert Museum, South Kensington, London SW7 2RL. Telephone: 01-589 6371, ext. 316 or 258.

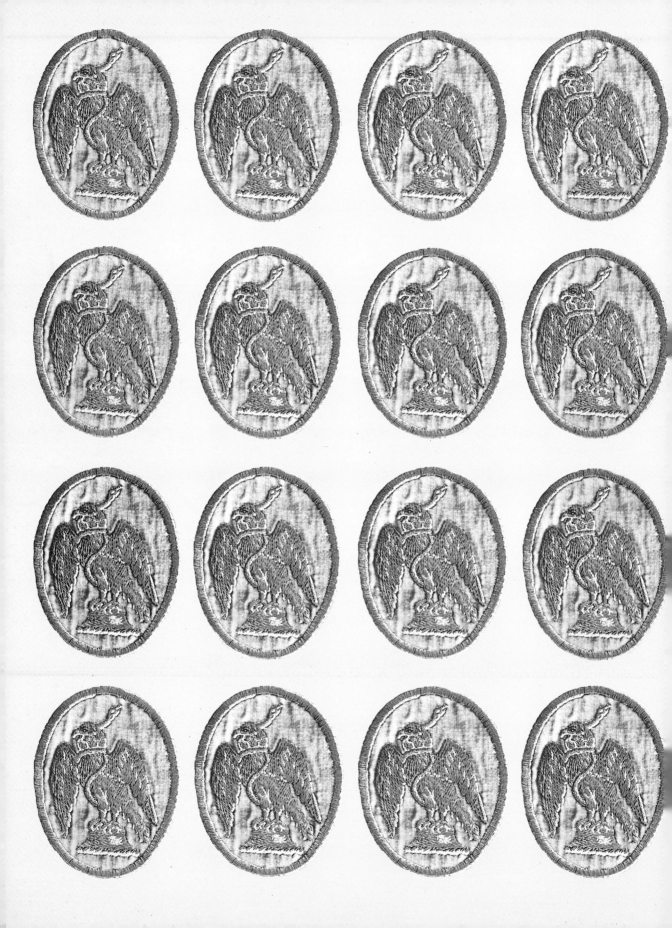